STEAMING

To Dan, my backer

NELL DUNN

STEAMING

"Live like a Warrior!
I've told you already, a Warrior
Takes responsibility for his acts.
For the most trivial of his acts."

Carlos Castaneda

AMBER LANE PRESS

All rights whatsoever in this play are strictly reserved
and application for performance, etc should be made
before rehearsal to:
Curtis Brown Literary Agents
4th floor, Haymarket House,
28-29 Haymarket, London SW1Y 4SP

No performance may be given unless a licence
has been obtained.

First published 1981,
reprinted 1982, 1984, 1985, 1988, 1991, 1995 by
Amber Lane Press Ltd,
Church Street, Charlbury, Oxford OX7 3PR
Telephone 01608 810024

Printed and bound in Great Britain by
Bocardo Press Ltd, Didcot, Oxfordshire

ISBN 0 906399 30 0

Steaming was first performed at The Theatre Royal, Stratford, London E.15, on July 1st, 1981, with the following cast:

VIOLET:	Jo Warne
BILL:	Stewart Harwood
JOSIE:	Georgina Hale
MRS MEADOW:	Maria Charles
DAWN:	Brenda Blethyn
NANCY:	Ann Lynn
JANE:	Patti Love

Directed by Roger Smith
Designed by Jenny Tiramani

The play transferred to The Comedy Theatre, London, on August 20th, 1981, with two changes of cast:

NANCY:	Sheila Ruskin
JANE:	Meg Davies

Characters

VIOLET:	about 45
JOSIE:	about 34
MRS MEADOW:	about 65
DAWN:	her daughter, about 35
NANCY:	about 38
JANE:	about 38
BILL:	a man who is heard but not seen

ACT ONE

SCENE ONE

*The 'Turkish' Rest Room of a 1909 Public Baths.
Green fluted columns and delicate ironwork contrast
with the new dilapidated beds and 'Turkish Lounge'
written in modern fancy lettering across one wall.
There is a sunken tiled bath with steps leading down
into it. This is the cold plunge. To one side is a small
table with some knitting and a radio on it and an arm-
chair. A row of metal lockers along the other side. In
the middle is a large old-fashioned weighing machine
and next to it a full-length mirror. Rain turning to
sleet beats against the glass skylight.*

VIOLET *comes in carrying a pile of towels. She puts
these down and busies herself getting the place ready
— plumping pillows on the beds, etc. The hiss of the
kettle on a little gas stove. She sings along to the radio
and looks round with some satisfaction. She disappears and reappears looking irritated — goes to one
side and shouts:*

VIOLET: Bill! Bill! Come down here!
　　　　　[*A man's shadow appears behind a glass
　　　　　door.*]
BILL: [*off*] What do you want?
　　　　　[VIOLET *turns off the radio.*]
VIOLET: The bloody showers aren't working again.
You promised me you'd get Maintenance to
see to it.

BILL: [*off*] I've reported it to Maintenance — they'll be along next week.

VIOLET: Next week's no good to my ladies — how can they relax without a nice hot shower? How can they wash their hair?

BILL: [*off*] Don't ask me. It's not my fault.

[*The shadow disappears.*]

VIOLET: This whole place is falling to bits and all you can say is — it's not my fault. It's always the same after men's day.

[*The door bursts open and* JOSIE *comes in.*]

JOSIE: Hello Violet!

VIOLET: Hello love —

JOSIE: I'll be truthful, I'm sick to death of buses — I've got my mink coat on, my jeans, my boots — but I've got no gloves — so I took a pair of bright blue socks and I've put them on my hands — they do look good.

[JOSIE *looks at herself in the mirror.* VIOLET *goes about her business.*]

VIOLET: Still with the foreign fellow?

JOSIE: [*beginning to undress*] Yes and you know what? I've got me rollers in me hair, a long night-gown, long pink socks, the top of a pair of pyjamas and he still wants to fuck me! He shouts at me, "Take them off now!" He shouts in his German accent, "Take them off now!" And he likes to rip them off! And he really hurt ripping off my suspenders — brand new they were and I can't wear them now. [*As she undresses she admires herself in the mirror.*] He hasn't got any friends — he never does anything exciting, he doesn't even want a car. It's automatic, his life — get up, get dressed, go to work, come home, have dinner, have a wash, watch telly, have a screw — that's the only thing he does like, sex, every night, loads of it

— I'm even getting sick of that, and you know me... [*gloomy*] ...I love sex!

VIOLET: I don't know why you don't get yourself a decent bloke.

JOSIE: Where do you find them? You tell me and I'll be straight round there.

VIOLET: You can't have my husband!

JOSIE: There you are — so I'm stuck with my Jerry — he's sat there and he's said, "I'm bored". "Oh, so you're bored are you?" — and I picks up his shirt — "Well, I'll give you something to do" — and I've taken his shirt ... [*She does the gestures*] ... and one by one I've twisted off the buttons — one, two, three, four — "There you are," I said, "Now go and sew those back on, that'll give you something to do!" Well, he's just looked at me — stared at me — like this ... [*She gives a mad cold stare.*] ... then he says, "Do you like snow?" "Not much," I says. And he goes to the cupboard and gets out this big bag of flour and scatters it all over me kitchen — it's gone everywhere — well, I just laughed, but he didn't laugh, he just sat and stared at me while I cleaned it up! What does he want out of life — you tell me, I mean we're not little kids, so what does he want? There's no joy there — I got this beautiful second-hand bench and I've painted it up — he didn't like it. I see this beautiful red dress — bright red with a red scarf to match — £40 — that's the dress I want, I says — he doesn't buy it. Jean can get anything off a man ... what's the matter with me?

[JOSIE *is now naked and arranging her bed.*]

VIOLET: If your purse is empty, put something in it.

JOSIE: That's what I'm trying to do. Look at it my way — he sleeps in my bed he's entitled to pay my bills. When I'm in debt like now it's as if only half of me were here — the other half's going round and round in my mind, shall I pay the L.E.B. or the telephone bill, if I sell that carriage clock I might be able to settle the gas bill — round and round, it drives you mad — I can't relax, I'm getting these terrible headaches. If I couldn't come here I'd go mad.

> [*She lies on her bed and* VIOLET *covers her with a warm towel.*]

VIOLET: There's only three ways you're going to get money — One: you inherit it — that's out! Two: you marry it, and Three: you earn it!

JOSIE: Well, three's out. What can I do?

VIOLET: You can get a job, my love.

JOSIE: What, in Boots? I'd go mad with boredom, you know I would.

VIOLET: Well, go on being skint then and living off fellers who ain't no good to you.

JOSIE: He'll have to pay my bills — I'm not a greedy person am I? It's just I haven't got it.

VIOLET: Now where have I heard that one before?

> [*The door opens.* MRS MEADOW *comes in followed by* DAWN.]

MRS MEADOW: My poor Dawn, slipped on the ice on her way out to the toilet — she's got a bruise as big as a coconut on her ... [*She presses her lips together at the unutterable word and taps* DAWN *on the bum.*] Then yesterday she missed the step — eh Dawn, been up to your gym again, drunk and disorderly, look at that! [*She pulls* DAWN*'s institution fringe back from her white forehead to reveal a bruise.*] My poor Dawn, I never can discover what she drinks when I'm out ... I've never found where she hides the empty bottles ... [*She smiles whilst* DAWN *bursts into wild laughter.*]

This'll make you laugh. [*to* DAWN, *who is still laughing*] Shut up, Dawn, and go and get undressed! I gets up this morning and there's snow all down my staircase.

VIOLET: Your roof leaking again, Mother Meadow?

DAWN: What do you think of my hair, Violet?

MRS MEADOW: I was in a hurry. It'll have to do! I've only got my kitchen scissors.

DAWN: Does it look all right? She won't let me grow it.

MRS MEADOW: She might get lice if she grows it. She always had short hair — what does she suddenly want to go and have it long for?

VIOLET: You've got to get someone to see to that roof or you'll get pneumonia!

MRS MEADOW: No. I've always been a lucky person. It'll probably stop when the weather gets better, besides it'd frighten Dawn to have a man climbing about on the roof.

DAWN: Might fall through!

MRS MEADOW: Don't be cheeky, Dawn — go and get undressed. [*in a loud whisper*] She's on her period, that's why she's acting funny ... always go funny when they're on their period, that kind of person.

DAWN: I had a lovely dinner yesterday: roast chicken, roast potatoes, bread sauce, cauliflower ...

MRS MEADOW: Gravy ...

DAWN: ... gravy, and then Mum made an apple pie for afters.

MRS MEADOW: We did enjoy it and then just as we're finished, Bernice arrives. "Why can't you put your knife and fork straight when you've finished eating, Mother?" she says. "I'm not interested in cutlery," I told her, "It's the dinner I enjoy."

DAWN: I'd like a couple of chops for tea.

MRS MEADOW: You're not having chops, Dawn. Bernice says

you're too fat. Go and weigh yourself. [*to* VIOLET] Every pound of extra weight takes a year off your life.

DAWN: I'd like a nice couple of chops. I must have something for my tea.

MRS MEADOW: She had a piece of fried pork with an egg on it for breakfast and three cups of tea, then straight after it she eats a whole box of jelly babies, so she can't have no more! Look at this!

> [MRS MEADOW *lifts* DAWN's *jumper and shows us her stomach straining against her pink nylon slip.* DAWN *smiles with pleasure at the attention.*]

DAWN: Oh go on Mum, I'm hungry!

MRS MEADOW: Shut up, Dawn! Terrible strain on the heart, always eating! [*She lifts her own jumper.*] See, I'm wearing my stays and my long woolly vest. I won't go out without my stays on even on the hottest day. I don't feel as if I've got any protection, it's like having nothing on without me stays. [*She rolls her eyes.*] You never know what people are thinking when you're out ... When Bernice comes, it's 'do this do that'. You wouldn't think she was coming to see her own mother and her sister, more like a health visitor. Come on, Dawn, get undressed!

> [MRS MEADOW *and* DAWN *pull the curtains shut around one of the beds. The door opens and* NANCY *comes in. She is warmly and sensibly dressed, with style. She carries an umbrella. She stands by the door and takes her boots off.*]

NANCY: Hello, is Jane here?

VIOLET: No, love.

NANCY: [*looking at her watch*] It's eleven o'clock — she said she'd be here by eleven. I'm meeting her.

VIOLET: I haven't seen you here before.

NANCY: No. I've never been — but I've heard about it from Jane.

VIOLET: Oh yes, Jane loves a good steam-up — well, here you are, take this bed and I'll put Jane next to you. Any of the lockers with the doors open are free. [*She hands her two towels.*] Take yer things off and have a go in the steam while yer waiting.

NANCY: Thank you, I think I'd rather wait for Jane to show me the ropes.

VIOLET: Oh yeah? You an old friend, then?

NANCY: Yes, we were at school together. [*turning away*] ... I'll just take my coat off, thank you!

VIOLET: [*looking* NANCY *up and down, not unkindly, but matter-of-fact*] I knew this woman who had thirty-five wigs and fifty pairs of sunglasses — the only time she was seen without them was when she came here...
[*She walks away.*]

NANCY: Oh!...
[*She goes to a locker and puts her boots and umbrella in it, then goes back to her bed. She takes out her face cream, anxiously looks at her watch and glances at the door, then takes out a book and begins to read. She ignores the other women.* MRS MEADOW *and* DAWN *emerge from behind their cubicle curtains, both dressed from head to foot in semi-transparent pink plastic and flowered bath caps, with flip-flops on their feet. They make for the scales.*]

MRS MEADOW: [*to* DAWN] Come on, up on the scales. Get up, we'll see how you're going.

DAWN: I'm not going to go back to skipping, whatever Bernice says.

MRS MEADOW: You'd better go and have a good steam-up, Dawn, you've put on three pounds since last week.

DAWN: It's me hair what's grown!

MRS MEADOW: No it's not, it's all them jelly babies you've been eating.

DAWN: [*laughs*] Never mind, Mother, you still love me, don't you?

MRS MEADOW: [*pretending not to hear*] Go into the steam, Dawn! Go on! Hurry up! Or I won't buy you a Tango for your tea. [*to* VIOLET] I haven't been feeling so good lately, my doctor gives me pills, don't do no good. He doesn't know my body — he hasn't time.

DAWN: [*from across the room*] You look rather yellow, Mother.

[*She laughs.*]

MRS MEADOW: Get in the steam, Dawn! She needs to sweat the acid out of her. [*in a conspiratorial whisper, rolling her eyes from side to side and turning her back towards* DAWN] She's been hearing the policemen again — she thinks they're hiding in the next-door garden watching her. When the police tried to get Dawn certified, one of them came to me and said: "What your daughter needs is to get married and have a baby". "You would say that, you big bully," I said. "You think that's all we women are here for, to satisfy your pleasure, don't you?" It's these four policemen, Dawn keeps seeing them. We've always been a decent family and kept ourselves to ourselves. I never let my children play in the street.

VIOLET: She was a normal girl till she got the job clerking at the station. I remember her passing the baths every morning — dot on 8.30 a.m.

MRS MEADOW: She could even ride a bicycle.

VIOLET: Something must have happened. Why didn't you ever ask her?

MRS MEADOW: Daddy was alive and he didn't like nothing

like that discussed. Don't bring it up, he'd say
— she'll get over it. Sent her to her room to lie
down — the doctor had given her tranquillisers
— That was in 1965 — she's been lying down
ever since except when she's eating or coming
here.

VIOLET: You ought to take her shopping with you.

MRS MEADOW: She won't go, you know that — hasn't been
out for sixteen years, except to come here.
Well, it's only a hundred yards and then she
tries to run ... No, Daddy didn't like anything
like that talked about ... he was a gentleman.

> [JANE *arrives. She is colourfully dressed in a jumble sale bohemian style.*]

JANE: [*shaking her wet hair*] God, I'm cold!

VIOLET: Hello darling, you'll soon warm up in here...

JANE: Hello Violet.

NANCY: Hello Jane

> [*They kiss quickly on the cheek.*]

JANE: Sorry I'm late! I was late getting up, late getting Sam off to school.

NANCY: Oh, your coat's really wet.

JANE: Can I hang it over your radiator?

VIOLET: Yes, dear.

> [JANE *hangs her coat up by the radiator.*]

JOSIE: I was just having this lovely dream, not sure if
I was dreaming or if it was a fantasy. Blood-
red silk, a pool of red silk and white silk curtains,
my body was slipping from side to side on this
blood-red silk and I pretend everybody is
watching me.

VIOLET: The showers aren't working.

JOSIE: Oh no!

JANE: I must wash my hair — it's disgusting!

VIOLET: I'll get you a bucket of hot water from the tap.
Maintenance are letting this place fall to pieces.

JANE: [*taking her clothes off*] Let's get undressed and

I'll show you around. I hope you haven't been
waiting long.

> [NANCY *begins undressing, looking around
> nervously, folding up her clothes very neatly.
> She knots a towel tightly around her and then
> takes off her knickers from under it.*]

NANCY: No, not long — but oh, Jane, thank God
you've come — I've had a lousy morning.

JANE: What's up?

NANCY: The washing machine's broken!

JANE: [*humorously*] Oh dear.

NANCY: The man promised to come yesterday — I
waited in all day.

JANE: And he never turned up?

NANCY: No... [*looking around her*] And to top it all, this
morning Nina was sick on my bedroom
carpet. [*distractedly*] Poor Nina, she's sixteen,
and if I don't chop up her food small enough
she's sick.

JANE: Bad as a baby.

NANCY: Yes, but I'd be lost without her. Oliver split
up with his girlfriend because he says if he's
going to be at university in York what's the
point of a girlfriend in London — and he won't
even be able to see her at weekends.

JANE: Tell him from me that he doesn't have to give
up his girlfriend ... at his age I had half a dozen
love affairs going—

NANCY: [*smiles*] You and your wild past...

> [VIOLET *arrives with a bucket of hot water.*]
> [*catching sight of herself in a mirror*] Oh God, all
> these mirrors — I look hideous!
> [*She looks away.*]

JANE: Can I borrow some of your face cream?

NANCY: Sure. It's Lancôme, on special offer at Peter
Jones.

JANE: You and your special offers. Look, I've

brought some *expensive* shampoo — avocado
— want to try some —?

NANCY: I didn't think I'd bother to wash my hair.

JANE: Oh but you must — the thing here is to get
completely wet and sweaty and dry and then
all wet again — it makes you expand — when
we're hungry Violet will get us something to
eat — when we're tired we'll lay on the beds
and sleep — come on, I'll show you round.

NANCY: Is it safe to leave my bag?

JANE: Take out everything you need and put your
clothes and your bag in your locker — then
we'll go and shower before the steam — Oh
hell, the showers aren't working —

VIOLET: Here's your water, Jane. Take it in the steam,
your mate can wash your hair.

JANE: I need a good steam-up. I was in a thoroughly
bad mood all weekend. There's something a
bit demoralising about being a mature student
and living on a grant at thirty-five — I had an
essay to do, which I just didn't feel like doing
... then Sam's bike got stolen and that upset
him ... and me ... finally, on Sunday, an ex-
lover of mine was coming to lunch and I'd
cooked this beautiful stew ... when he didn't
arrive I rang him up and he'd completely
forgotten and was about to go and see his
father...

NANCY: What did you do?

JANE: I told him ... it didn't matter a bit — I'd only
made stew ... and anyway I had an essay to
write. Then I put the telephone down and
burst into tears.

NANCY: Do you miss living with a man?

JANE: No I don't. At least not the ones I've lived with
... When I went to California last year it was
really great being with women who are into

women. Trouble is, I fancy men.

NANCY: I wish I knew what I fancied. I don't think I've thought about what I *wanted* for years. Oh blast, that reminds me, I forgot to empty the vinegar out of the decanter.

JANE: What?

NANCY: It was stained — you know you get stains out of cut glass decanters by filling them with salt and vinegar.

JOSIE: Well, that's handy to know.

[MRS MEADOW *appropriates the bucket.* JANE *and* NANCY *go into the steam.*]

MRS MEADOW: [*dipping her flannel in*] Come here, Dawn! I never use shampoo, it's a waste of money. I get my flannel and I rub a bit of Palmolive soap on me flannel and then I wet my hair down and rub it with the soapy flannel then Dawn pours a jug of water over me head. But I much prefer it here when I can get under the showers. I've lived there since 1924 and I've never had hot water. But then I'm lucky because if I had hot water — I'd be like Josie, always worrying about the bills and I wouldn't get the company I get here. Dawn and I look forward to coming here all week.

VIOLET: Do you, darling?

MRS MEADOW: This is our big day.

DAWN: It's boring all the other days.

MRS MEADOW: You shut up you — you get well looked after, don't you?

DAWN: It's boring.

MRS MEADOW: Go and lie down, Dawn, your legs look a bit white. [*to* VIOLET] Can you do my corns? My feet are nice and clean. I've given them a good scrub and chucked a bucket of clean water over them.

[VIOLET *sits beside her.*]

Not all the neighbours are good, you know. One old woman down the street said she'd seen Dawn singing in the Red Lion — yes she did, said she'd seen her drinking gin and attempting to sing through a microphone. My girl would never go into a pub.

DAWN: [*calling out from behind the curtain*] There's somebody looking at me, Mother!

MRS MEADOW: Shut up, Dawn! [*to* VIOLET *in a confidential whisper*] She lay in bed for three days, the sweat coming off her like a pint of milk, from head to toe. I know something happened down the station, but someone said to me, "You'll never win against the police force — they'll all hang together and swear no-one touched your daughter." The doctor gave her tablets but the tablets made her sleepy. Of course, Dad went up to Scotland Yard once or twice. The Superintendent told him, "If we ever find out one of our men interfered with your daugher he'll be severely reprimanded." I wish I could go in one day and find her dead in the chair. I hope she dies before me. Of course, I'll miss her but if I go who'll look after her? I've felt a bit tired this week — I've had two early nights — Dawn was pleased, couldn't wait to jump into bed with the bottle — it was half past six we went to bed last night.

[*She pushes her false teeth in and out of her mouth with her tongue as she talks and she looks swiftly to left and right in case we are being overheard.*]

I suppose it's a bit of love and a bit of duty that made me stick to her. But I am her mother!

[NANCY *and* JANE, *wrapped in towels, emerge out of the steam and make for the cold plunge.*

They stand on the edge, take off their towels, then NANCY, *holding up her hair with one hand, walks down into the ice-cold water, up to her knees. Suddenly* JANE *runs down the steps past her, catches her by the hand and pulls her in. They both tumble into the water, shrieking, splashing each other and ducking down under the water.* VIOLET *appears.*]

VIOLET: Now ladies, not too much fun or the Council will close me down!

[NANCY *and* JANE *come up out of the cold water.* VIOLET *hands them towels.*]

NANCY: Oh, it's warm!

VIOLET: Give yourselves a really good hard rub.

JANE: Turn round.

[NANCY *turns her back and* JANE *rubs it.*]

Arms up!

[*She rubs* NANCY *from behind, right down her body.*]

NANCY: Luxury!

JANE: Let's have a cigarette. I'm so beautifully warm. My flat's freezing!

[*They sit on a wooden bench and light up.*]

JOSIE: [*walks past*] I wish I dared get in the plunge.

JANE: It's not deep.

JOSIE: I'm frightened of water. I never learnt to swim as a kid. I'm frightened of putting my head right under.

JANE: I stayed up till four this morning doing an Islamic history essay — I feel quite high. At eleven I was in tears about it. Then I said to myself, "Work Jane! Work! And this time next year, with a first class degree in Arabic, you will be taking tours in a little steamer — up the Nile, lecturing on Middle Eastern history."

NANCY: I had an amazing dream last night — I had been given a baby girl to look after — she wasn't mine — I put her in a tumble drier and forgot her. A woman came to tell me she was dead. I couldn't bear to look at her dried-up shrivelled body. I asked the woman to wrap her in a brightly coloured towel to make her look better — "You will have to tell her mother, she is coming to see her today." I was so frightened I would be blamed for the dead baby. "Anyway, she was deformed," I said, "So perhaps they will be glad she is dead." Then the clean brown towel I was going to have her wrapped in was balanced on the bonnet of a remote control heavy-muck digger which suddenly moved and the towel fell in the mud and I wouldn't be able to *hide* her ... mud everywhere ... a sea of mud ... my terror that it was all my fault. The woman didn't blame me, only that it had happened and I must face it. Jane, I was the baby and you were the woman — you didn't make me feel guilty.

JANE: What are you guilty of?

MRS MEADOW: [*to* VIOLET] I picked some of my chrysanths for you and brought them into the house — they were all being eaten by creepy-crawlies. Made me shiver all over.

[*She undoes a newspaper package.*]

DAWN: [*still teasing*] I think you must have met someone, Mother, you're all red around the mouth and chin — you've met someone while you've been out — own up!

VIOLET: They're beautiful — I'll go and put them in water.

MRS MEADOW: Go and weigh yourself — go on!

[DAWN *lumbers off.*]

I'd sooner fly in the air than leave her alone — It's a policeman — he came round swearing Dawn had torn his coat to pieces. She knows all their beats — what time all of them are where, and she hasn't been out for sixteen years. Never did find out what happened, but one thing's for sure — Dawn wouldn't have led anyone on. No, my Dawn's never even kissed me. We're not a kissing family. Don't believe in it — so how come she could have led a policeman on? As for my son, I've never asked my son for anything. Never even asked him to carry the coal when he was a lad and working for his exams — But now he's got his own business I'd like him to sit down with me and Dawn — she is his sister — he must have some feeling for her — just sit down and have a meal with us. I suppose he's ashamed of us but Dawn's not a bad girl. Because she's been to the nerve hospital it doesn't mean she's bad.

[DAWN *is in the background, repeating what her mother is saying.*]

DAWN: No, he could sit down and have a cup of tea with me — it's only my nerves, I'm not bad — never did nothing to no-one.

MRS MEADOW: Between you and me, Arthur wouldn't look after Dawn if anything happened to me. I've asked him and he says, "No, she'll have to be removed — she'll have to go away," he says, I could have killed him.

[MRS MEADOW *goes off towards her bed,* DAWN *follows her.*]

Go into the corner and skip, Dawn.

[DAWN *takes up the rope and begins to skip, singing a skipping song, the rope whacking against her plastic-covered legs.*]

DAWN: Mademoiselle from Armentières, parley-voo!
She's never been kissed for sixteen years, parley-voo!
The Prince of Wales was put in jail
For riding a horse without a tail
Inky pinkie parley-voo!

NANCY: Were you surprised when I got in touch?

JANE: I came to the wedding, you know — saw the little nineteen-year-old lamb go to the slaughter. At least I waited till I was twenty-five — I wrote to you once.

NANCY: I know, I never answered. I didn't know how you'd take to William.

JANE: Or how he'd take to me?

NANCY: He wouldn't have liked you.

JANE: Why not?

NANCY: Because you always say what you think! I'm going down to watch Oliver play tomorrow — he's captain of the school rugger team!

JANE: Proud Mum!

NANCY: I was hopeless at sport. Remember the time I let the whole side down by dropping the ball at the crucial moment in the rounders match against St. Hilda's, and Clodagh Morrison swung me round the changing room by the hair? I was so furious.

JANE: But you wouldn't show it!

NANCY: My mother said, "Ladies never raise their voices" — but you rescued me!

JANE: I always liked you from the day you arrived and — much to everyone's amazement — fitted into a two foot square locker with the door shut — you were determined to succeed at something!

JOSIE: Here Jane, you come from a good home, is this normal? He had it six times the other night and he got up after every time and went and had a wash and he expected me to do the same. I was trooping back and forth all night — mad bastard, I'm wore out —

JANE: [*laughing*] No, it doesn't sound exactly normal to me.

[NANCY *is clearly embarrassed.*]

JOSIE: He made me wild last night, we was having it and I was really getting into it and enjoying it, when he's come. "Hold up!" I says, "What about me?" Well, after that I made him plate me for an hour till I came, every time he lifts his head I push it back down — I wouldn't even let him up to breathe... I can feel it from the bottom of my toes to the top of my skull. It's as if something pealed right through my body ... I hadn't come like that for months. It did me the world of good.

MRS MEADOW: My cat's been out for two days — he's never done that before.

VIOLET: Well, I shouldn't worry, perhaps he's found a girlfriend.

MRS MEADOW: Oh no, he's not interested in that, he's been doctored.

DAWN: [*echoes*] He's been doctored.

MRS MEADOW: But it could be the toms are making his life a misery.

DAWN: [*teasing her mother*] You look a bit yellow, Mother!

> [DAWN *goes into wild laughter.* MRS MEADOW *totally ignores her and goes on talking.*]

MRS MEADOW: A friend of mine once had a neutered tom and there weren't any females in the area so all the local toms made his life a misery and took him for a female — made his life a misery.

NANCY: [*looks at her watch nervously*] What's the time?

> [*The shadow of a man is seen magnified on the glass door. A* MAN*'s voice:*]

BILL: [*off*] Violet!

> [DAWN *sits up with a start.*]

DAWN: The police! The police!

MRS MEADOW: Oh shut up and lie down, Dawn!

VIOLET: It's only Bill.

MRS MEADOW: [*to* DAWN] Take two of your pills and go back to sleep — you gave me a start.

[VIOLET *goes out*.]

NANCY: [*nervously*] I must get dressed and go. [*She hurries*.] I'm late.

JANE: Stay — I'm not going to hurry. Sam's having tea with a friend today.

NANCY: No, I've got loads to do and Nina to let out — Benjy will be wondering what's happened to me...

JANE: Come on Nancy, relax, Benjy can look after himself.

[*Minutes later*. VIOLET *reappears*.]

VIOLET: He's not going to upset me — all because I know too much about him — when I caught him having breakfast with his fancy woman and the Manager comes down and tells me there's all the towels to be sorted out in 'The Swim'. I says to him, "Come here, Mr Bidette, and tell me to my face, after I've done all the towels in 'The Turkish' you want me to go and do all the towels in 'The Swim' when Bill Bradley is sitting in there eating egg, bacon and beans with his fancy woman" ... "Oh no," I says, "You men may stick together but you're not having me wearing myself out!"

MRS MEADOW: What's going on?

VIOLET: Says the boiler's corroded and he's going to turn off my hot water supply at seven o'clock.

JOSIE: He can't do that, we'd all freeze — what does he think we come here for? If I want to freeze I can freeze at home.

VIOLET: Says the boiler's out of date.

MRS MEADOW: I'll give him out of date — he'll be saying I'm out of date next —

DAWN: [*teasing*] Throw away your old bag, Mother — you mustn't hoard, old people hoard — shows you're getting old!

MRS MEADOW: Shut your mouth, Dawn, and keep skipping, nobody asked you to speak.

VIOLET: Off to the pub every dinner time, staying till three o'clock when he's meant to be taking care of the place, he wouldn't get away with it if he were my old man. "Tell Maintenance to order a new boiler," I says, and he laughs in my face. "Cost near on £75,000 to modernize this place," he says — "So what?" I says. "That's what the rates are for, aren't they? I suppose they expect us to go to Monte Carlo for a 'relax' do they?"

[NANCY *meanwhile is hurriedly dressing.*]

SCENE TWO

A week later

VIOLET *is no longer wearing her white coat but instead a fancy one-piece bathing suit — she is down on her knees mending a leaking pipe with lagging.*

BILL: [*off*] Women. You're all the same. Make out you're almighty and directly something goes wrong it's ... [*in a woman's voice*] ... Help! Help! Bill! The pipe's leaking! Quick! Fetch a hammer! Do this! Do that! I've had plenty of experience of women and it all adds up to one story — you're only happy laying on your backs — eating chocolate! [*Silence.*] Violet! Violet, are you there?

VIOLET: Go away, Bradley, I'm occupied!

[*She turns the radio on.* MRS MEADOW *and* DAWN *come in, wet and cold.*]

MRS MEADOW: I didn't mean to come today, I haven't been feeling myself again, and Dawn's back so bad.

DAWN: My back's aching. I've been bailing out the water.

MRS MEADOW: Shut up, Dawn, they don't know what you're talking about. We've got this tin bath — it holds a lot but it's been full all week and when it overflows it comes through the ceiling on to the floor below, so Dawn has to bail it out with a tin into a bucket then she can carry the bucket downstairs.

DAWN: And empty it in the garden —

MRS MEADOW: Haven't got a sink upstairs — snow all down the stairs and then it thaws in the sunshine. At night it freezes and the stairs are covered in ice. Of course, we never go up there.

DAWN: Except to bail out.

MRS MEADOW: Keep quiet you and get undressed. She had one of her arguments with three policemen in the kitchen this morning — you should have heard the things she was accusing them of — coming through the skylight spying on her from next door — wanting her to — Oh! She was angry! [*in a whisper to* VIOLET] I love my Dawn, nobody's going to take my Dawn away from me.

DAWN: [*from her cubicle*] What are we having for tea, Mum?

MRS MEADOW: A couple of gold fish fried in hair oil!

DAWN: Oh Mum!

MRS MEADOW: [*in a whisper*] I've got a leg of lamb, fresh mint in the garden, what the frost hasn't killed, roast potatoes and carrots. Then we'll have a nice lie down after tea with the hot water bottle. The other afternoon me and Dawn had a lie down on the bed — we just take our shoes off and get under the counterpane — the hot water bottle between us. Next thing I know, I wake up, it's pitch dark — I look at the clock — it's midnight — there's the two of us lying under the counterpane, fully dressed!

VIOLET: [*getting up from the floor*] Now that's fixed, I'm not having Bill pretending he can't turn the hot water on today because the pipe's leaking.

MRS MEADOW: [*pushing her false teeth in and out with her tongue*] My fire's not burning too well — the chimney sweep's been and it's still not burning properly. I reckon the people next door have stuck something down my chimney —

[JOSIE *bursts in.*]

JOSIE: He's gone. Taken everything. Only thing left is one pair of shoes under the bed. He even took his towels and the toothpaste — couldn't even clean me bleeding teeth this morning. How could he have just walked out like that after fourteen months? He found out about the job. "I can't live with you," he says, "You're a slut," and he packs his stuff, rips my clothes off my back and wallops me. [*She pulls up her skirt and shows the bruises on her thighs.*] I called him a German cunt — he went mad — called me a prostitute, ripped off my clothes and hit me in the mouth. My lip's killing me! How can I go to the club like this? I've got to have excitement or I die. I looked at him last night, he asked me to go for a walk, what do I want to walk down to the river with you for I'll end drowning myself! He hated it!

[*She starts crying again.*]

VIOLET: Go and get in the steam, darling.

JOSIE: I know you're going to tell me I ought to get myself a job and stand on my own feet, but what can I do? I couldn't stand the sort of job I could get. I couldn't stand the boredom of it, I'd go mad. I want someone to look after me!

VIOLET: Hard to find these days.

JOSIE: He can't have just walked out like that, can he?

VIOLET: Well, my love, he has, so he can. Now it's happened — you'd better face it.

JOSIE: Even rolled up the carpet in the front room and took it with him. [*crying*] What's going to happen to me now, Violet?

[JOSIE *drops on her knees and lays her head in* VIOLET*'s lap.*]

VIOLET: Right now you're going to take your clothes off and have a good steam-up.

JOSIE: I went down on my knees to him Violet. I begged him, I even said: "I'll try and stop swearing" — I've got a terrible feeling it's come up from deep down inside me — it's a horrible feeling ... I'm all choked up. I was going to me new job ... He said, "Your place is in the home" ... "I haven't got any money," I said. He slung twenty pounds at me. See, my wrists are all bruised from banging my arms against the wall.

VIOLET: [*holding* JOSIE*'s wrists*] Look, it's starting to snow! Snow!

JOSIE: The trouble is, I know it's hopeless but I want him back more than anything, I want him back.

[JOSIE *and* VIOLET *look up at the skylight. It is snowing.*]

I've got to find a job or I'll starve.

SCENE THREE

A week later

JOSIE *is plucking her eyebrows in the mirror.*

JOSIE: At least my body will be admired and not abused! "Who do you think you are?" He says that to me whenever I look good! I've got this boil come up just under me left tit, what shall I do? The club's topless and I've just got to wear seamless tights and this blood-red shawl round me waist. Jerry will kill me if he finds out about all this — thank God it's an afternoon club. I used this bleeding Helena Rubinstein suntan on me face — you should have seen me — fucking hell — I looked like a bleedin' Pakistani with blonde hair — all I needed was the turban — anyway, they took me! I must earn some money ... What if all the girls are young girls and nobody wants to talk to me? ... What if they notice this boil under me tit? I'll have to disguise it. I'll buy meself a bit of flesh-coloured silk chiffon.

VIOLET: That'll cost you a few bob.

JOSIE: I know I'm extravagant with clothes but that's me, I've always been like it.

VIOLET: My daughter's like you, "That's old fashioned, Mum," she says ... years gone by ... We'd all spend Christmas together ... the whole family get together for Christmas tea ... it's not like that any more ... she does it posh now ... a few people round for punch, I feel out of place ... she worries about what I'll wear.

JOSIE: You've got lovely kids and not one of them in Borstal, you're lucky, Violet.

VIOLET: If anyone ever says to you — "Isn't Violet lucky — she's got four lovely kids," you say to them — "I sweated blood in every moment of their growing — if they're any good now it's because I taught them," — and my God they did some dreadful things — the time Brian stole my Aunty's wedding ring while she was asleep. "I know you've done it, Brian," I said, "And unless you give it back this minute you

and I are going down the police station."
Well, that cracked him — he knew I meant it
and did he holler — they must have heard him
all the way to the Town Hall.

JOSIE: My poor little boy stuck in an approved school
at fifteen — just like his Dad. What about your
kids, Nancy?

NANCY: My eldest son is about to go to university, my
daughter's at boarding school and my youngest
is about to go to his public school.

JOSIE: So you're well pleased with yourself.

NANCY: Well, not exactly.

JOSIE: I bet you did it all *just* right. Always in bed early
to make sure you're up to cook the kids' breakfast in the morning.

NANCY: Yes — [*suddenly thoughtful*] — but sometimes I
resented it.

JOSIE: Oh yeah?

NANCY: I never said so ... but once they *all* forgot my
birthday — the whole family and I didn't
remind them, I just thought to myself — well,
you'll all grow up horrible people — and it will
serve you right.
          [JOSIE *laughs.*]

VIOLET: I never gave way to my kids — I always knew
I was as important as they were — so I didn't
let them take no liberties. "No," I said, and I
stood my ground — they knew where they was
— I didn't have to do a lot of screaming and
shouting.

JOSIE: It must be wonderful to have a baby with
someone who really wants one ... here, let me
help you with the towels.

VIOLET: My husband said, "I'm not going to be left
out," and he hasn't been — came in from the
beginning, even chose the nappies with me.
I'd feed, he'd change ... [*Sexily*] ... lovely times

in the middle of the night...

JOSIE: I wish my Johnny had gone to university instead of Borstal.

VIOLET: When I told my mother I was getting this job — she was still alive then — "You won't like that job, Violet, working with naked bodies!" But she ended up coming here herself and loving it.

JOSIE: Perhaps if I were more like you, sensible, he would have done.

VIOLET: I started eighteen years ago and I got ten pounds a week for a 40-hour week. That was good money — I'd been working in a clothing factory on piece work and you were always rushing and tearing — you couldn't stop for no dinner and there was so much thieving — six gross of buttons disappeared one day — the foreman was so frightened of the women he didn't dare accuse them in case it started a fight!

JOSIE: But all he knows is thieving.

> [JANE *comes out of the steam and jumps into the plunge.*]

Is your husband well off, Nancy?

NANCY: We were pretty hard up when we were first married. William hadn't gone to the bar yet — I wrote down everything I spent — my father was a lawyer and he taught me to balance my books — we were given bank accounts at fifteen. It was pain of death if you were a penny overdrawn!

> [JANE *arrives out of the plunge, all wet, and rubbing her hair.*]

JANE: Oh, don't talk to me of bank accounts. You know my father was a bank manager. Just after I was married he got very ill, whether it was to do with the marriage I don't know, and we drove down to see him in our old banger. Well, there he lay on his death bed and I tiptoed in to see him and all he said was, "Is your car taxed and insured?" That was the last time I saw him conscious.

[JANE *lies on her bed and oils herself.*]

JOSIE: [*to* NANCY] So you've never been in debt?

NANCY: No!

JOSIE: [*with genuine fascination*] Well fuck me! That's the first time I've met someone who's never been in debt!

[*A pause, while* NANCY *is gathering her courage.*]

NANCY: My husband left me!

JOSIE: I'm sorry.

NANCY: Last summer. It was early evening, we were going out to dinner — I'd ironed my frock — it was one I adored, I'd had it for ages — with a Victorian lace bodice — I got it at Laura Ashley's when it first opened — I was resting, William was a little late home — he came upstairs and sat on the edge of the bed — the magnolia outside the open window was in blossom. "I've fallen in love with someone else," he said. "I want to leave." He left that night, after twenty-two years. I remember looking at my frock hanging on the door and wondering what I'd done wrong.

JOSIE: Life will always hurt you — so what's the point of being responsible?

NANCY: I tried to make him happy.

JOSIE: Didn't you take up with anyone else when he left?

NANCY: You can't 'take up' with anyone with a twelve-year-old boy in the house.

JOSIE: Why not?

NANCY: He'd be so upset!

JOSIE: We might as well've not been born as to be always sensible —

    [NANCY *rummages in her wallet and takes out some photographs and hands them to* JOSIE]

NANCY: My house!

JOSIE: Now that's just the sort of place I'd like — look at all the windows, it must have a load of rooms!

NANCY: Yes, far too many.

JOSIE: I lived in a museum ... the whole time I was with my husband ... all we ever talked about was the house and the furniture. It was bent stuff anyway — when I wasn't talking about it I was polishing it ...

    [*She makes polishing gestures.*]

DAWN: [*from the weighing machine*] I've lost five pounds, Mother!

MRS MEADOW: [*ignores her*] Finding a decent man is as hard as finding a needle in a haystack. My husband was a good man but that's because he was seventeen years older than me and I was his baby.

DAWN: [*playing with the brass weights*] Look, Mother, I've lost ten pounds.

MRS MEADOW: No, he never interfered with me after Dawn was born. Go and lie down, Dawn, you need plenty of rest!

    [JOSIE *is stretched out on her bed.*]

JOSIE: I'd just like to lie there and have people pay to come and look at me — I wouldn't have to move a muscle, just lie there in the nude and you'd pay to come and have a good look.

DAWN: I'd like to do that too but Mother wouldn't let me take my plastics off.

MRS MEADOW: Don't you dare, Dawn!

DAWN: [*to* JOSIE] Bernice tore up the Love Book you brought me — she tore it up and threw it in the fire ... she called me an idle slut...

MRS MEADOW: Don't tell stories about your sister ... [*changing the subject*] I drink three glasses of water a day, it keeps me flushed through, your system must need a good flush out every day mustn't it? And I take a vitamin daily ... never forget that. I get up about six a.m. and make a cup of tea for myself and Dawn then she takes her tablets and goes back to sleep till nine but I get up. I like the early morning summer time, it's too cold now. But in the summer I go and water my garden ... they wouldn't give me a garden if I moved ... I'd rather have a hole in the roof than leave my garden.

JOSIE: [*conspiratorially to* DAWN] I'll buy you another one next week.

DAWN: Oh thank you, Josie, don't tell Mother.

[JOSIE *begins to sing some happy love song —
she looks at herself in the mirror.*]

JOSIE: Do you know what my Mum said to me the other day? She said my arse was bigger than hers! Well, I could have died. "Your arse, Mum, is twice the size of mine." "It's all according to how you look at it," she says, "I stick out more in front because I've had so many children..." Well, that *really* got on my nerves.

[*She is admiring her body in the mirror.*]

MRS MEADOW: My cat's been out all night, he hasn't eaten for two days. I don't know what he's been up to. I'm going to give him a tablet.

JOSIE: [*musing, still looking at herself*] I'd die without my clothes and my make-up — I've never really got over that time I lost a trunk of my best clothes coming back from holiday in Tenerife with Big John. I can still remember every single stitch of clothing that was in that case.

[JANE *is lying on her bed asleep.* NANCY, *who*

> *has been lying on her bed, gets up and goes towards the steam.* JOSIE *catches her as she passes.*]

Here Nance, you can't see if that's a little spot I've got on the back of me neck can yer?

NANCY: [*looking*] I can't see anything...

JOSIE: Here, look at you in the mirror...

NANCY: [*shutting her eyes*] God, is that face really mine?

JOSIE: You're not a bad-looking woman. A lot of men would fancy you ... go on, take a look at yerself. [NANCY *looks.*] Another thing, you're tall, where I'm only little and that gets on me nerves sometimes because I always have to wear high heels...

NANCY: [*looking at herself*] Horseface!

JOSIE: I've got some cucumber cream at home, it's supposed to shrink the bags under your eyes. I'll bring you some in next week ... not that you hardly need it.

> [*She inspects her own 'bags'.*]

NANCY: [*turns and looks at* JOSIE] Thanks, but just at the moment it feels more than cucumber cream I need.

JOSIE: Oh, so that's it, well, whatever you want, my love, you go ahead and get it. I can't stint me-self. If I don't get what I want, I'm miserable!

NANCY: [*musingly*] And do you always know what you want?

JOSIE: No, I don't ... sometimes I feel all anyhow and I couldn't care less ... but mostly I know...

JANE: [*wakes up and stretches*] Know what? God, that was a beautiful snooze...

NANCY: I asked Josie if she knew what she wanted...

JANE: And what did you say, Josie?

> [JOSIE *breaks into some song ... such as 'Come on baby light my fire' — Shirley Bassey. She lies down by the pool.*]

NANCY: This morning I was listening to Richard

Strauss. You know, the record with Elisabeth
Schwarzkopf singing 'Four Last Songs'. I was
upstairs — I've taken the gramophone up to
my bedroom — it used to be in the sitting
room and it was always William who chose
the music we played — I lay on the floor —
and then as I listened — suddenly a feeling of
space like the night sky, and I cried out "Ah"
... so long since I'd felt such utter loveliness
and peace. [*Pause.*] When we were first married,
William made me walk about naked. He said I
had the most beautiful body he'd ever seen.
He refused to let me be shy, he took hundreds
of photographs. [*Pause.*] It's funny, really, I
look at my face and I see this intense woman
with staring blue eyes and unfamiliar face ...
look at me, Jane —

> [JANE *puts her arm round* NANCY *and her cheek
> against hers and they go on staring in the
> mirror.*]

JOSIE: [*still by the pool*] I hate responsibility. As long
as I can find somebody to keep me why should
I go to work? I'm really hot now. I'm lying
nude by a river and a man in a beautiful white
suit who I've never seen before comes and
kneels at my feet and begins to kiss them,
kisses me all the way up my body ... ahhhh ...

SCENE FOUR

A week later

NANCY, JANE *and* VIOLET *appear with a hammer —
they've been inspecting the boiler. They're dusty.*

NANCY: There is not a leak or even a sign of one!
JANE: That water tank isn't dangerous!

VIOLET: Load of rot! I'm not having Bill Bradley lie to me. I bet on the men's day they have the steam on till nine o'clock at night and nobody talks about leaks. I shall have to go to the Town Hall myself and see Maintenance.

[DAWN *bursts in.*]

DAWN: Mother's not well. She told me to come. I've come on my own.

JANE: Good for you.

VIOLET: What's the matter with Mother?

DAWN: Sick! It came up like a fountain. I had to run and fetch a great big bowl.

NANCY: When was that?

DAWN: Yesterday and last night when we was laying in bed — the lights was dim — she says, "We are born to die."

[*She cries and brings her skirt up to her eyes to wipe her tears.*]

NANCY: Don't cry, Dawn.

VIOLET: Let her have a good cry ... [*She takes* DAWN *over to her bed.*] There you are, darling, take yer things off — lay on the bed and have a good cry ... Is mother sleeping now?

DAWN: She told me to come. I didn't want to leave her but she says, "I don't want you hanging around me, Dawn. Violet will make you a sandwich."

JANE: [*to* DAWN] I'm going in the steam in a moment, want to come?

DAWN: [*sobbing*] I want to have a good cry.

JANE: The steam's a good place for crying. Has she seen the doctor?

DAWN: No, but Bernice came over ... [*She starts crying again.*] ... she called me an idle slut and said Mummy won't get better no more and she'll have me put away ... She was angry with me because I couldn't open the tin. She was angry

because the milk was still on the step at half
past ten! ... She doesn't understand, does she?

[*She goes to her bed to have a good cry.* VIOLET
tends her. JOSIE *comes in all dressed up and
wearing dark glasses.*]

VIOLET: What on earth are you wearing?

JOSIE: Look at my face! [*She takes off the glasses and
reveals a bruised face.*] He done that last night.
He'd been drinking. He put his hands round
my throat and said, "I'm going to kill you."
"You're touched," I said. "I'm going to gas
you," he says in a horrible deep voice. "Don't
be silly," I says, "Let me go." But inside I was
really scared. "Get on the bed," he says. "No,"
I says. "I'm not going to have nothing to do
with you." So wallop, he hits me — I don't
know what happened next! ... It all started
because I was wearing a new dress. "Now
you've got your job you think you're the only
woman in the world! Ha! Ha!" he goes. "I suppose you think you're a beauty queen? Ha!"
My poor ear, how come I always get hit on me
left side?

NANCY: Why on earth did you take him back?

JOSIE: "Don't throw dirty water away till you've got
clean," my Mum always says.

[*No-one speaks.*]

[*angrily*] How am I going to pay my bills? It's
all very well for women like you, you can
afford to live without men — I can't! At fifteen
I was going early morning cleaning with my
Mum! At sixteen I was having a baby ... You
were still at school. [*Pause.*] I'm sick of poverty.
Guess what time I worked till? From Saturday
night I worked till seven o'clock Sunday
morning on the boats, barmaiding — seven
o'clock in the morning and I earned £30.

NANCY: That's wonderful.

JOSIE: It wasn't wonderful — it was bloody hard work but at least I got my rates money. When I got home I sat down in a chair and fell fast asleep. That was Sunday and now what do you think came through me door this morning? Another fucking bill — this time for me television. I don't see why they keep sending me all these bills — it does me nerves up trying to pay them when I'm on me own ... He hasn't been near or by for a week.

> [*Everyone is silent.* DAWN *is listening to* JOSIE *with fascination. Pause.*]

Well, Sunday afternoon I was so tired I wore these old jeans and socks and guess what? *He* turns up! [*imitating* JERRY] "You look disgusting, you have let yerself go. No-one will ever look at you if you dress like that." Oh, I was choked! I was so choked, I thought is it really worth it, my struggle to stand on me own feet? [*to* VIOLET] So I took him back. "One day I'm going to kill you," he says. Then we has it, but it didn't do me no good so after he'd gone I got me Pifco out. I had to. I had so much tension in me it was like a screw going round — the back of my neck. "Books," he says, "Read books." "I can't read books, they bore me. Books, books, books, I'll look like a book one of these days — I want a bit of life not books." I want to be somebody, to have done something. At the moment all I'm going to get on my gravestone is: "She was a good fuck!" I don't want to be remembered just for that.

VIOLET: There's plenty haven't even been remembered for that.

> [*A silence.* VIOLET*'s gas ring goes out. The kettle stops hissing.*]

Me bleeding ring's gone out.

[*She tries to light it and fails. She goes to the bottom of the stairs.*]

Bill! Me bleeding gas isn't coming through to me ring.

[*A pause. Then he shouts:*]

BILL: [*off*] The pipes are corroded. It isn't safe to let the gas through.

VIOLET: [*shouting back*] I'd like to see you and sort this out. [*She comes back in.*] Bleedin' nuisance. He's meant to keep this place in order — this place was built as a luxury for working people — not a shit house!

[*The shadow of* BILL *is seen in front of the door.*]

BILL: [*off*] Can you come up here a minute? The Manager wants to see you.

VIOLET: Well he'll have to see me in me bathing suit, I'm not getting dressed.

[*She goes out.*]

NANCY: So why are all men shits?

JANE: It's weakness, it's weak. Because it's easier to be a shit — it's easier not to bother to say what you're going to do — not to ring when you say you're going to ring — not to arrive when you say you'll arrive — it's easier to move on.

JOSIE: To tell you bleedin' lies every time they open their bleedin' mouths.

JANE: Well, we mustn't let them be shits — we mustn't let them get away with it. It's our fault we let them get away with it!

NANCY: Why? Why do we let them get away with it?

JOSIE: They think they're so important!

JANE: [*with scorn*] Mothers who do everything for their sons.

NANCY: Yes ... perhaps it's us ... when my first baby was born — I remember the nurse saying "Wake up, dear, you've got a son!" I can still remember the sense of thrill at those words —

I kept repeating them to myself all that week, over and over, and each time I was thrilled — I may only be a woman but I had given birth to a male and that for me was ultimate success.

JANE: You see, we've got to believe we really are as important as they are, not better, not worse, but just as important! It's as if men haven't cottoned on to how exciting it could be to know a woman really well.

JOSIE: [*suddenly softening*] Well, my love ... that is a thrilling moment in any woman's life ... you had your first kid...

NANCY: Yes ... just for a while I felt a real woman ... but most of my marriage I was just trying to make up the sort of person who did everything right ... even in bed ... it didn't occur to me I could ask for what I wanted...

JOSIE: So you never told him how you really felt? ...

NANCY: I did try telling him once and he said, "Don't upset me now, I've got a very heavy work load on."

JOSIE: You shouldn't have let him get away with that ... You should have yelled at him ... "What are you then, a man or a toad! ... You're supposed to be my husband and I'm your wife!" That's what I used to say to my old man ... we'd have a row and then we'd make it up and he'd cuddle me up and say, "Josie, I love you" ... if he hadn't got done for the jewellery robbery and got sent down for fifteen years ... I'd have been all right.

JANE: Quite frankly, I don't think most men are worth bothering about.

JOSIE: What would we have to get excited over, eh?

NANCY: Benjy went off to school today, with his great big trunk!

JANE: Oh Nance, you never said!

JOSIE: You all right, love? I know you was dreading it.

NANCY: Odd thing, but I am all right. I live in a desert but right now I feel at peace here, it's a peaceful desert ... just me ... and Nina ...

JOSIE: Good for you.

DAWN: Do you think I could try the steam without me plastics on?

JANE: [*going to sit beside* NANCY] I don't know how I'll feel when Sam leaves home, pretty lost, I dare say, for a while.

JOSIE: Come on, love, come in with me, you can help me wash my hair.

DAWN: Shall I weigh myself?

JOSIE: No, don't bother about nothing. Get out of yer plastics and come into the steam. [*She sings.*] 'Help me through the night ... Lay down by my side do.'

> [VIOLET *reappears, shattered. The conversation stops. She walks over to her chair and sits down.*]

Here Violet, you all right?

DAWN: What's the matter, Vi?

VIOLET: ... Eighteen years ... and only six weeks' notice.

JANE: What?

VIOLET: After eighteen years here with all my ladies ...

NANCY: What's happened?

VIOLET: They're closing our baths!

JANE: The bastards!

VIOLET: We've only six more weeks.

> [VIOLET *lays her head on her table and weeps.*]

JOSIE: [*goes over to her*] My poor Vi, what a bloody cheek!

VIOLET: They shouldn't be allowed to take that decision without consulting me!

NANCY: Did they tell you why?

VIOLET: The Manager says they're going to build a branch library. I had one hundred and twenty-three customers last week — he says they say that's not enough. It was enough in 1960, why isn't it enough now? He says the Council says people want libraries more than baths. He says the place is obsolete.

JOSIE: Well, we're people aren't we? Where am I going to go to have my fantasies? Anyway, my flat's freezing — I'd go mad if I stayed there all day.

DAWN: Won't Mother and I be allowed to come here any more?

VIOLET: People shouldn't make decisions over and above the heads of them that are responsible for it. I know more about these baths and who comes here, and why, than all the councillors put together ... What about my blind ladies? What about Mrs Meadow and Dawn? How are they ever going to manage? ... They're closing this place on lies! I'm not having it closed on lies!

[*The truth has reached* DAWN. *She gives a great shriek and then bursts into very loud sobs.*]

END OF ACT ONE

ACT TWO

SCENE ONE

MRS MEADOW *is ill in bed in one of the cubicles. They are surrounded by notices saying things like "These Baths should be Saved!", "No More Free Baths for O.A.P.s if These Baths Close", "What do they take us for, Mugs? IS IT BECAUSE the Council is only interested in Politics and not People", "Back to the Old Days, Two Buckets A Leg in Each Bucket to Have a Bath", "First to go was our Hospital, then our Market now our Baths unless you STOP IT! SIGN OUR PETITION!"*

NANCY *and* JOSIE, *wrapped in small towels, are in the forefront of the stage, sitting cross-legged opposite each other.*

NANCY: Ma mi Ma Moooo Ribena ... Rolls R-R-R.

JOSIE: [*repeats after her*] Ma Me Ma Mooo Ribena Rools.

NANCY: Ro R-R-R Rolls. Where's your tongue?

JOSIE: Rools.

NANCY: Rolls!

JOSIE: Rolls!

NANCY: Yes, that's it, well done!

JOSIE: [*falls backwards onto her back*] Can I have a rest now, I'm done in! Rolls! Rolls! Rolls!

NANCY: That's great!

JOSIE: Wow, you're better than the fellow who run the evening class, he said my tongue was very stiff and I must open my mouth wide to loosen my tongue muscles ... He was an actor, only a young fellow ... wanted to come round one night when I told him Jerry had left me. So I've dressed up in my black fringe knickers and I've put a black scarf round me neck and me ...

NANCY: My.

JOSIE: And my gold necklace and I've lit a candle.

NANCY: [*laughing*] Josie!

JOSIE: I felt like it! When he looks at me — he's got beautiful eyes — I can see into every part of him. That next day he was still turned on, but I said, "No, enough is enough."

NANCY: How do you do it, Josie?

JOSIE: They're like stallions when they're young — fantastic to have it off with a young fellow if you're hot-blooded. If you fancy him — have him. And don't feel guilty about it — you've got to have a fling sometimes ... or you'll just get old and boring.

NANCY: [*thoughtfully*] Yes.

JOSIE: Well, my love, you must borrow my Pifco ... I had it going this morning from five past eight till five to nine and I had this beautiful fantasy — I was fucking meself and I thought I was so beautiful I was in love with meself ... *my*self ... Oh, I hope I haven't done *my* back in, I'm exhausted. I'm going to lie down and go to sleep in the Hot Room!

NANCY: I'm jealous!

JOSIE: I tell yer ...

NANCY: *You.*

JOSIE: I tell you, I'm going to fetch it for you later ... [*She gets up and stretches.*] I see stars — I come from the top of my head to the back of *my* heels ...

[*She walks off.*]

MRS MEADOW: [*from behind her curtains*] Violet!

VIOLET: Yes, love.

MRS MEADOW: There's a horrible snake-like thing climbing over the window ...

VIOLET: That's my Russian vine, grown like a lunatic that has — all the cold in Siberia can't kill him!

MRS MEADOW: It writhes when the wind blows ... it's making awful wriggly shadows against the glass and I'm sure it's full of slimy things, slugs and insects, all slimy ... I don't know how you can bear it ... making me feel worse ... I wish I'd stayed at home.

VIOLET: What, in this weather, are you mad? You'd have froze to death. Now you just shut yer eyes for a bit and I'll make you a nice cup of tea and a sandwich.

MRS MEADOW: My daughter Bernice couldn't come and look after me because this titled lady had come and asked her to look after her highly pedigree dog ... she had to do it.

DAWN: She called me a selfish pig! She slammed the door in my face and called me a selfish pig. I'm not. I'm keeping the house clean. She's very unkind, my sister!

[JOSIE *shows* VIOLET *her new coat.*]

JOSIE: I know I shouldn't but I wanted it, that was all there was to it.

VIOLET: It looks the business! [*to* DAWN] She is and all!

JOSIE: [*to* VIOLET] I find it very difficult if I want something not to have what I want ... I have to have things because it satisfies something inside me.

VIOLET: What you can't pay for, darling, you can't have.

JOSIE: Thank God you don't have to pay for sex ... it was terrific Friday night. I was like a raving bull. I haven't had such good sex for a month

... He's been wonderful to me since then ... damp-proofed my front room ∴ tiled my kitchen ... It's beautiful, so darling that's me and how are you? ...

VIOLET: The council phones through last night to say the chimney's dangerous and they're sending the architect down to have a look. I had a ladder all ready for him. "I can't go up there," he says, "I suffer from vertigo." "You're not going up?" I says. "No," he says, "I'm not." So he looks up it with a pair of binoculars ... it's black as night ... "You can't see no cracks up there, can you?" I says. "No, I can't," he says ...

MRS MEADOW: I've been using the baths for thirty-eight years ... I don't look all that old but I am ... and if they close the baths I'm going to cry my eyes out ...

VIOLET: Who wants a bleedin' library? They've got a library round the corner.

MRS MEADOW: She wouldn't go to the library, there's men go there, what would she want to go to a library for?

VIOLET: They can do what they like these days and live off the fat of the land. This used to be a lovely place to live, look at it now.

JOSIE: I want a library so I can educate myself — get a good job — I'm sick of shit work.

VIOLET: When I was a girl there used to be timber barges, fruit barges, sugar barges. My Mum used to work in the Hospital, night work. They've closed that. My Dad used to work in the Brewery, they pulled that down. Now my brother works in the West End and lives in Kent — he's up at five — leaves home at twenty to seven in the morning, he doesn't get home till late. I say this — they should open up the canals and rivers — the cafes were open all night — this place was alive then.

MRS MEADOW: The ten-wheelers rushing through — they destroy people's nerves. [*opening her locker*] Violet, there's a man from Billingsgate been using this locker!

JOSIE: I might even write a book ... my friend out at Sutton told me in her new library they've got live writers writing there in little cells — you can go and visit them and tell them your story and they'll show you how to make them into best-sellers.

MRS MEADOW: Dirty, dusty books. This is the only place Dawn and I get any social life — I mean, you can't *talk* in the library, can you? Big notices everywhere saying SILENCE.

JOSIE: I like clacking my high heels in the library — click-clack, click-clack — makes everyone look up. Look at the hairs on me legs. Last time I shaved them I used Jerry's razor — he went mad, said it was disgusting — threw the razor away.

VIOLET: My husband never objected to me using his — "What's the point of having two when one will do?" he says.

JOSIE: Well, he's going to have to do my passage. I'm going to have it all done in new wood.

VIOLET: Have you told him yet?

JOSIE: Yes, I told him — "Oh no," he says, "It'll look too small!" "Look," I says, "I don't care if it looks like a rabbit hutch, I can't afford a damp course and I'm not going to have mould growing in my passage!"

[JANE *arrives, looking very excited.*]

JANE: I've got news! Straight from the Town Hall. The Council have agreed to call a special meeting of the Leisure Committee. Councillor

Sellars is going to present our petition — Friday evening at seven o'clock.

NANCY: Splendid!

JANE: Right, well we've only two days to get organized — loads to do. [*She goes across to the table, taking off her coat as she goes.*] Have you seen the headlines of todays Chronicle? [*holding out the paper*]

VIOLET: [*taking the paper, reads:*] "Save our Baths. The Baths in Trigate Road are under Threat of Closure but the ladies of the Turkish are on the warpath. Four weeks before the building is to be officially closed by the Council, 'Save our Baths' campaigners got going and put the Turkish under siege with their petition!"

NANCY: Wow! Sounds like Napoleon.

[*The women stand around excited.*]

MRS MEADOW: I hope it doesn't mention me or Dawn. My Bernice wouldn't like it! "Drawing attention to yourself, Mother," she'd say!

JANE: These are some of the facts we have to put across to the public ... There are 9000 homes without baths in the borough, 25,000 O.A.P.'s who can't afford to run a gas heater. Two hundred blind who need assistance to bath ... This is the procedure to be followed. [*She reads from a printed paper.*] "In accordance with Standing Order 29 (d) a deputation shall be comprised of persons who signed the request and shall consist of not less than three or more than ten persons; they may appoint another person to act as their spokesman. Only one member of the deputation shall be at liberty to address the Committee and the speech of such Member shall be limited to fifteen minutes."

JOSIE: They don't half try and make it sound complicated!

JANE: Well, give me half an hour to muster the facts ... then we can make decisions!

[DAWN *meanwhile has taken off her plastic mac and, looking in the mirror, has painted her nipples red.*]

NANCY: Hey, that looks great Dawn!

JOSIE: Wow!

[*She whistles.*]

MRS MEADOW: What you doing, Dawn!

VIOLET: Drink yer tea, darling, she's only painting.

MRS MEADOW: Well, I don't want her getting no paint on her plastics!

NANCY: She won't!

JOSIE: [*to* VIOLET, *helping her*] If I work in the topless club three nights a week that's £15 — then I get £30 from him — that's my food paid and my electric — then if Celia pays me what she owes me that's me telephone — she got married on the rebound — she'd only known him two weeks, now he wants it four times a day and he keeps all the food locked up in a suitcase, the poor cow, oh aren't I lucky ... you don't know how lucky you are till you see how other people live! Now I've only got me car to M.O.T., license and insure then I'm in the clear.

NANCY: Life's difficult for everyone at times.

JOSIE: Well, my life's just survival ... I even had to wank the fellow off to get the club job in the first place.

JANE: You didn't have to, you chose to.

JOSIE: You sounded just like my teacher.

JANE: Sorry! God, I've run out of paper!

[*She leaves.*]

JOSIE: She wore flat shoes and a tweed coat — She hit me once with a ruler and I ran home and told me Mum. She come up the school and slapped the teacher. They chucked me out — I'd have

to have left anyway the next month — I was
pregnant!

NANCY: [*thoughtfully*] Jane's right, Josie — you didn't
have to — you chose to.

[JOSIE *faces* NANCY.]

JOSIE: What do you know of it anyway? ...

NANCY: I know you have to pay for self-respect.

JOSIE: What sort of a job can I get? I'm not even a
young girl any more. And I happen to like nice
things ... I like money ... I don't like wearing
'sensible' shoes and last year's coat and organ-
ising other people's lives like a colonel-in-
chief. Well, I'm going to tell you something —
I don't *want* to be like you. It's boring, it's
every day! Boring! Boring! Boring! Do you
know why us working-class women have a little
bit on the side? Why we spend money on
clothes and make-up and shoes when we
don't, as you say, 'strictly need them'? We've
been brought up to do the shit work and we
can't escape from doing the shit work except
by finding a man with money and hanging on
to him! Anyway, who's to say you've got a
better life than me? — I'm not so sure — I've
been to South Africa, the Barbados, Tenerife
— I've laid beside more pools than you've had
hot dinners!

NANCY: On stolen money?

JOSIE: So what? You don't thieve because you don't
need to, not because you're any better than I
am! I want excitement in my life! I want beautiful clothes, beautiful travelling, cars ... if I've
got to steal them — well, at least I've had
them, which is more than I can say for you.
Have your drab dreary life and keep your
good name if that's what you want. Women
should be beautiful things of pleasure. [*She*

walks away then turns back.] Do you know what it feels like to go into a library if you don't know your way around ... and you get looked down on because of your accent?

NANCY: Looked down on?

VIOLET: The only time I ever went in the library was when I was caught out ... dying to go I was ... flew in there and asked for the toilet ... "You'll have to ask the Chief Librarian," he says. The Chief Librarian, a woman — I thought, well, surely she'll have a bit of sympathy for me — "No," she says, "Staff only." "Why's that?" I say. "Bomb caution," she says, "Bomb caution?" I says, "I only want to go to the toilet."

JOSIE: [*ignoring* VIOLET] They think too bloody much of themselves. Real facts in life are what you feel and what you experience — those are facts, facts aren't what you read in books.

NANCY: [*shaken*] Look down on? I've never looked down on you. That's simply not fair!

JOSIE: It's a horrible feeling being looked down on — being turned down for job after job because you haven't got the qualifications ... because you can't spell and you can't speak right ... and you know in the end all they're going to offer you is cleaning!

NANCY: [*has stood up*] ... Please stop!

JOSIE: Why should I stop when you tell me? ... Who are you ... Miss Boss? Just because you can spell you think you're Queen of England ... well, you're not ... you're just an ordinary woman with a bit of money who's been deserted by her old man — I'm not surprised he left you — you always have to be on top! You pretend different deep down that's how you are — he wanted loving not organizing.

NANCY: Shut up — bloody well shut up!

> [NANCY *puts her hands over her ears and turns her back.*]

JOSIE: I haven't finished yet ... You should have heard the things *he* said to me — "You'll end up a waitress by the time you're forty." Perhaps it's true, perhaps it's true and I just can't stand it! I can't stand poverty. "You're a nobody!" he says, "You'll never get anywhere!" In the last six months I've been to eighteen interviews, I've lived from day to day like any dog or cat, driver, receptionist — they don't like my accent — sales rep ... I've tried them all ... what did I end up with — 'Radio Rentals', after taking half an hour on the 14 bus that never comes and sitting all day on me own in the back room answering the phone ... if you think that sort of job gives you self-respect I'll tell you about last night when I goes for this job in the club. "You've got such a beautiful skin, Josie, please take your clothes off." "Well," I thought, "I may as well," so I've took me top off and I've sat there and he's touched me tits "What beautiful tits you've got!" There I was, sitting in that poxy club with me tits all hanging out, and a fellow I didn't even fancy with his hand up me skirt. And I've screwed up me eyes and then I thought, "What on earth am I doing this for? Ten bleeding quid and a job," and I felt sick — He took his trousers and his socks off and he spreads one of them Advance towels on the floor and wants me to lie down on it. I screwed up me eyes tight and I said, "Come on, Josie, you need the money!" but inside I felt sick, I felt cheap —

> [*Everyone is quiet.* JOSIE *looks around.* NANCY *takes her hands off her ears and listens.*]

When I was married I was a skiv ... I'd still be
a skiv if I was with him now, the same thing
day in day out, do this, do that, that's security.
Well, I'd rather be living off a man. I may be
skint but I've lived ... I *can* do what I feel like,
that's something you'll never be able to do ...
If I want to go out and get drunk ... I go.

> [NANCY *turns back.*]

If I want to stay in bed in the morning I stay
there — and if I want to fuck I fuck, whereas
you — you daren't take what you want. [*She
shrugs her shoulders.*] I lost me temper! [*She looks
around.*] It's spending too much time with
women — I've always preferred a man's
company. [*She walks away and then turns.*] I wish
I could get rid of my anger. I feel so angry all
the time with everyone who has let me down
— I am so bitter about having nothing.

> [*Pause.* NANCY, *catching some of* JOSIE'*s
> anger, but as if talking to herself:*]

NANCY: Do you think my husband ever encouraged
me? He never encouraged me to do anything,
not even to make friends ... if I brought someone new to the house ... he'd criticize them,
when they'd gone, call me a lesbian! Make fun
of them ... the shoes they wore ... or what they
said ... I wouldn't ask them again. In the end
the only people who came to the house were
other successful lawyers and their wives. I
took on all his ways — slowly everything of me
got eroded ... You don't really know you exist
so then what possible use could you be out
there in the big wide world when all you know
how to do is to stay in and wait for the coal-
man, the gasman, the man from the LEB, the
man come to mend the washing machine, why
is it always men I wonder? — I suppose all the
women are waiting in, like me. And then every

day always be there when they get back from
school. Be there, otherwise you'll have 'neg-
lected children' who turn into delinquents
who steal and take drugs and end up dead
from an overdose ...

JOSIE: [*still challengingly*] And so?

NANCY: So nothing. I had an offer — but "Don't come
in with your arms full of love and warmth!
Stay away!" I hadn't the time or the inclina-
tion for that sort of thing!

JOSIE: Frightened?

NANCY: Yes.

JOSIE: Well, my love, we're all frightened ... every
day when I wake up you know what I pray for?
I pray for courage. And a good sex life! Every
woman has the right to a good sex life! Why
didn't you leave him?

NANCY: [*turns to face* JOSIE *and says slowly and deliberately*]
Perhaps I didn't leave him because I had a
lovely home, a lovely garden. I saw no way I
could keep myself and my children in the
manner to which we were accustomed ... I had
no money!

JOSIE: Oh ... you sound a bit like me!

NANCY: I've never realized that before ...
[*She bursts out laughing.*]

JOSIE: [*laughing with her*] Fucking hypocrite! Fucking
goodie-goodie two shoes! Fucking fairy on the
Christmas tree!
[NANCY *collapses into a relieved laughter
which is almost sobbing — an enormous sense
of surprise.* JANE *arrives back.*]

JANE: What on earth's going on?

MRS MEADOW: Fighting and showing off, that's what's been
going on!

JANE: Listen, I just had this idea while I was out —
Josie you'll have to be our speaker at the
meeting.

JOSIE: Me?

JANE: Yes, don't you see? Violet can't do it because it looks like she's just saving her job — Mrs Meadow and Dawn are out and Nancy and I — we wouldn't do it so well —

JOSIE: But I've never spoken before an audience in my life —

JANE: We'll help you prepare.

JOSIE: Not on your Nelly!

NANCY: [*challengingly*] Who's frightened now?

SCENE TWO

NANCY, JOSIE *and* JANE *are seated at the table, which is covered in papers.* JOSIE *has a pen in her hand and is wearing glasses.*

JOSIE: "The information being put out on behalf of the Council is making the public feel that the baths are unsafe. The Council's case is dishonest. There is no 'serious and irresponsible risk to public safety'. It is the published opinion of the technical officers that there is *no* immediate risk at all which would warrant a recommendation for closure."

NANCY: That sounds great!

JANE: Now, if you could follow that up with some figures — where's our calculator — about how much the council spends on, say, keeping someone in an old people's home compared to giving them a Turkish bath once a week for a year — that's so the audience can get to grips with just what it does cost to keep this place going ...

JOSIE: Hey, Nancy ... I'm getting nervous ... sure you shouldn't do the speaking?

NANCY: No ... you were born within fifty yards of these

baths, you know this district inside out — you're in a much stronger position and quite frankly I think you'll do it well.

JANE: You'll be all right tonight!

JOSIE: I mustn't swear and I mustn't get drunk. I'm going to wear my little patent leather black boots and my red patent belt!

JANE: Just give them the facts and follow it up by your own argument ...

[VIOLET *enters with her overcoat dripping and two large brown carrier bags.*]

VIOLET: I met this Jewish fellow outside, he said, "Violet, you've got the best steam in London! Gets all the acid that lingers ... acid's poison and your steam gets every ounce of poison out of my system!" So he gives me a fiver towards our campaign!

MRS MEADOW: [*with her eyes shut*] Jewish fellow did you say? I wouldn't get mixed up with them — ooooh no, I wouldn't get involved — you can never tell, can you? Oh, I'd be careful if I were you ...

VIOLET: Come on ladies, Indian take-away for six! Wake up Mother Meadow and put your teeth in. Today's the Big Day!

[DAWN *appears in the nude.*]

MRS MEADOW: [*opening her eyes with a start*] Don't be cheeky! I've had my teeth since 1949. When I was at the hospital the nurses kept saying, why don't you keep your teeth by your bed like everyone else? — "I didn't get these teeth to keep by the bed," I says. [*suddenly seeing* DAWN] Dawn! What on earth are you doing! Put your plastics back on! Hurry up!

DAWN: They say my body's beautiful!

[*She touches her breasts.*]

MRS MEADOW: I know what's making you so cheeky. You haven't taken your tablets.

DAWN: I'm not going to neither ... I feel nice when I
                 don't take my tablets. I've been looking in the
                 mirror while you've been sleeping!

MRS MEADOW: I hope you've been ashamed by what you've
                 seen.

DAWN: My body's nice!

MRS MEADOW: You're a wicked girl. Violet, draw my cur-
                 tains! The police will be after you if you're not
                 careful.

DAWN: No they won't, Violet don't allow men in here!
                 My skin's ever so white! Snow white!
                 [*She smacks her thighs.*]

MRS MEADOW: Don't answer back, Dawn. You're making me
                 worse.

DAWN: You're ill, Mother! Go to sleep! I like feeling
                 excited!

MRS MEADOW: Don't be so dirty — don't pay any attention to
                 what she says, overactive imagination the
                 doctor put it down to. Now take your tablets,
                 Dawn, or you won't get any dinner!

DAWN: Violet's bought me dinner!

MRS MEADOW: Oh you are a bad girl, close my curtains up, I
                 don't want to see you!

DAWN: [*gets her skipping rope and chants*] Don't play in
                 the street! Don't play in the street! Don't talk
                 to men!

VIOLET: Come on, Dawn! Stop tormenting your mother!

DAWN: I like feeling cheeky.

VIOLET: We all do but we don't talk about it at dinner
                 time.
                 [*In the background* VIOLET, NANCY *and* JANE
                 *are laying out lunch. The table is covered with a
                 cloth and plates and knives and forks.* VIOLET
                 makes a big pot of tea. JOSIE *appears, naked
                 and damp.*]

JOSIE: I've got a little ulcer right on the lip of my
                 beautiful fanny!

NANCY: I hope it wasn't anything to do with that elocution teacher.

JOSIE: I'll kill him if it was, I'll a-e-i-o-u him till he doesn't know what hit him!

[*They sit round the table in varying degrees of nudity and start to eat.*]

DAWN: [*wrapped in a towel*] What do you want, Mother, chicken or curry? I'll bring you a nice big plate.

MRS MEADOW: Put your clothes on first or you'll put me off my food! The trouble with you is you're getting too excited!

DAWN: I'll do you a lovely plate of dinner ...

[*She piles a plate full and takes it behind the curtains. The women tuck into the food with pleasure.* VIOLET *pours steaming cups of tea.*]

JANE: [*tucking in*] God, this is delicious!

JOSIE: This vindaloo hot, Violet?

[*A great delight in the feast ... a sensual pleasure that is allowed.*]

I'm enjoying this ... I like us all sitting around the table. I'd like to be a prison governor — in charge of a lot of people, someone important — not just some fellow's old lady! How about you, Jane?

JANE: No, neither marriage nor a regular job. I want to go back to being a traveller.

VIOLET: Won't be so easy with Sam.

JANE: Sam's a great traveller! He learnt to speak Greek when he was two and a half.

NANCY: What were you doing in Greece?

JANE: David had got involved in the boat charter business and we went to live on this Greek island in a tiny fishing village. Sam used to get up each morning and go down to this old woman's house and wait for one of her chickens to lay an egg so he could bring it back for his breakfast.

NANCY: [*enviously*] Sounds idyllic!

JANE: It was till David left and I ran out of money. I had to take a bus twenty miles to the nearest telephone to ring London. Then we missed the last bus home and I had to carry Sam on my back ... after about four miles I was nearly dead when along comes this man on a motor bike and we rode pillion through the mountains. Sam slept all the way!

JOSIE: Did you stay on, on yer tod?

JANE: For about a month — we did the grape harvest — but it's hard being a woman on your own in Greece. Once I woke up in the middle of the night to find a man in my bed. I'd left the window open, it was so hot!

[*All sing 'Strangers in the night'.*]

JOSIE: Dirty bastard! What did you do?

JANE: [*laughing*] I told him to go, of course!

NANCY: How terrifying!

DAWN: [*smiling*] I bet you liked it Jane, own up, don't tell no fibs.

JANE: He was one of the villagers. I think he thought he was on to a good thing!

JOSIE: And was he?

JANE: [*giggling*] All kinds of things can happen when you travel. [*seriously*] But I want *adult* company, but not marriage — even if I was in love I'd have to find some other way. When my friend Rose stayed the night — the next day was Sunday and we got up and made breakfast together — it was so lovely sitting at the table eating breakfast with someone else, not always just Sam and me.

JOSIE: But if it had been a fellow what had stayed, he'd have been sitting at the table and you'd have been cooking the breakfast.

JANE: It's our fault if we do that ... we shouldn't do it.

NANCY: We want them to think well of us ...

JANE: We want to impress them ... Super-Woman, Wow!

NANCY: That's the trap!

[*They lean across the table towards each other and kiss.*]

My husband used to invite his friends to dinner and they'd say, "I hear you're a wonderful cook!" So of course I'd have to live up to my reputation!

JANE: Well, I love cooking, but I don't intend spending much time in the kitchen on my own any more — if anyone wants a beautiful meal they can cook it with me!

JOSIE: Me too ... I'm sick to death of the kitchen ... I spent the best ten years of my life feeding my kid and my old man ... in he'd come, rubbing his hands, first thing he says, "What's for dinner, then?"

VIOLET: Funny isn't it, they go bald, they go impotent, but they never lose their interest in their grub!

NANCY: I always liked the nursery better than the kitchen. Then suddenly they've grown too big for it — they've burst the walls and they're striding towards you saying, "Now what?" and "More!" and "Where do we go from here?" And you don't know, so you run for cover, hands over your ears, shrieking, "Help me! Help me!"

JOSIE: They start talking of sex and money and ugly things like that.

JANE: ... and take drugs ... and try and commit suicide ...

JOSIE: They begin to steal cars and end up in Borstal.

VIOLET: They tell us we're old and badly dressed, and that we'll get cancer if we go on smoking ...

NANCY: They tell us they're unhappy and it's all *our* fault!

[*Pause.*]

VIOLET: One thing's for sure, they all leave home!

MRS MEADOW: [*from behind the curtains*] My Dawn hasn't! She likes it!

[*All laugh.*]

VIOLET: [*serving up*] Who's for second helpings?

NANCY: Me please!

VIOLET: To have done well by your kids, to send them out into the world knowing they're well loved ... it's satisfying ... it's one of the most satisfying things there are when I look at my kids and I'm proud of them.

NANCY: Me too!

JANE: I'm proud of Sam, too, but it doesn't mean just because I've got a kid I'm going to stop living. The longer you stay indoors the more frightening the outside world becomes.

NANCY: I want to be part of the world, not shut up in my house any more!

DAWN: [*tucking in*] Tell that to Mother! She won't like it!

MRS MEADOW: Dawn doesn't like going far. Never keen on school. She went on to summer camp once, but she didn't like it, wanted to come home. The others stayed but not my Dawn!

DAWN: [*calling to her*] Remember the Anderson shelter Mother! Daddy let me use it as a playhouse!

MRS MEADOW: Still see the foundations in the back yard ... In the morning I'd make the sandwiches to take down for a picnic tea. We took the shutters off the front room to use as bunks.

DAWN: Daddy fitted up a two-watt electric light.

MRS MEADOW: The cat come down with us.

DAWN: It was cosy!

MRS MEADOW: If Daddy was here we'd never have that hole in the roof!

DAWN: Perhaps it'll go away ... remember, Mother, we had that leak four years ago and it stopped all by itself.

MRS MEADOW: It'll probably clear up, roofs usually do.

DAWN: It was Daddy who was angry with me when I liked that policeman. .

MRS MEADOW: You never liked no policeman ...

DAWN: Yes I did, that's why I tore his jacket ... he wouldn't go out with me — blue serge it was and it had this funny smell when I tore it, it made this ripping sound ... it was that policeman what put his tongue in my ear.

MRS MEADOW: You're telling stories, Dawn ... no-one put their tongue in your ear.

DAWN: He did and all ... and more things he done but he wouldn't take me out ... so I tore his jacket ...

MRS MEADOW: Overactive imagination — where are your tablets? ... Violet, find her tablets, I don't know what she'll imagine next.

DAWN: It was lovely when he put his tongue in my ear. Daddy was very angry when I told him. Daddy didn't speak to me all week and it was my birthday. Daddy didn't say 'Happy Birthday' to me.

MRS MEADOW: The police come down to my house ... and wanted to put Dawn away ... I had to promise to keep her indoors ... his uniform was all torn.

DAWN: I liked his uniform ... he had a truncheon hanging on his belt.

MRS MEADOW: If I hadn't kept her indoors they would have put her away. She gets too active.

JOSIE: Let's light a candle and make the table all beautiful. When I speak at the meeting tonight I'm going to give them the facts and the figures then I'm going to make them a suggestion. If they was to give us a grant to do this place up we could do wonders. New beds and luxury towels, soft lighting for our rest room then — we could all get together and have discussions of how we all want to run the place and who's going to be responsible for what. I don't mean we'd take you over, Violet. You'd be the manageress and we'd be the committee!

VIOLET: Sounds a sensible idea to me, love, and I'll be right behind you tonight when I hear you stand up and say it!

JOSIE: Do you think we'd all fall out if we tried to run this place together?

JANE: Not if we worked at it.

NANCY: All relationships are frail.

JANE: With men they are! How is it one day you have so much intimacy that you have the right to put your hand in a man's pocket when you're out walking — to keep your fingers warm. A day later he's left you for another woman — it's not worth it — I'm going to settle for an interesting life!

NANCY: [*with humour*] Next time I'll write my own marriage vows ... I promise always to listen to you and to try and understand what you are saying. I promise to try and talk to you and tell you who I am.

JOSIE: Oh, that's beautiful! I shivered, I want to love Jerry — I want to feel my love for him real inside me — not a pretend love ... a real love with all my feelings ... How can you love someone if you don't know where they are, what they're up to?

JANE: Unexpected things happen when you tell the truth!

NANCY: I'd like that ... I'd like to be with a man, living with a man ... getting really close.

JOSIE: Sing and others join in the second time around.

NANCY: It's going to be pretty hot stuff! In the meantime I've got friends!

JOSIE: I've become wicked now — I want this scene

all silver and candlelight and blood-red lip-
stick with the light shining on it ... I'm wearing
these long silver stockings up over my thighs,
no suspender belt, just a silver chain around
my waist. Silver paper all over the floor —
candlelight catching the silver and I'm going
to stand there very dominating and tell him
what to do ... I'll make him plate me for an
hour ... I'll tell him everything ... I won't hold
nothing back ... I'll tell him how much I hate
him ... how much he put me down ... how
much he hurt me ... what a failure he is ... and
then after all that we'll have it!...

DAWN: Remember, Mother, we saw that lady dance
with the spangle in her belly button! [*cheering
up*] I remember it was at the Granville, Mother
and Daddy took me there for my birthday and
they had a woman in a jungle costume dancing
with a diamond in her belly. Mother thought
we should get up and leave but I started making
a fuss so Daddy told her to shut her eyes till it
was over.

JANE: Was it good?

DAWN: It was beautiful. She danced like this.

[*She gets off the bed, sways her body and
dances.*]

MRS MEADOW: That was Daddy's fault. Took you to the
Granville for the Christmas show. That was
the start of it!

[*The shadow of* BILL *appears against the glass
door.*]

SCENE THREE

NANCY *and* JANE *have stayed behind at the Baths.*
JOSIE, VIOLET *and* DAWN *have gone to the Council*

Meeting. MRS MEADOW *is propped up on her bed asleep.* JANE *is giving* NANCY *a massage.* NANCY *is lying on the massage table on her back.*

NANCY: When I got up in the morning she was lying on the sofa where I'd left her ... she must have died in her sleep ... Nina ... we got her when she was six weeks old and Oliver was two ... she was such a lovely dog ... my children grew up with her ... I don't think I can take any more change.

JANE: Put your fingers on your throat ... feel the little pulse there?
[*Pause.*]

NANCY: Yes.

JANE: Now move your hand slowly down your breasts to your ribcage.
[*Pause.*]

NANCY: It feels like a bird locked up inside me. I saw William the other day, the first time since the divorce. I said to him, "When we were married I was so lonely," and he said, "And so was I — so lonely." After the first year we could never look each other in the eyes.

JANE: [*pressing on* NANCY's *upper chest*] How does that feel?

NANCY: Better. Hey, I wonder how Josie's getting on, perhaps we shouldn't have sent her off like that.

JANE: Into the lion's den. Violet will take care of her. Here?
[*She massages* NANCY's *stomach.*]

NANCY: .Yes there ... sometimes I felt as if a whole pack of hounds were after me ... and so I worked harder than ever to make the house spotless and the food good and the bills low so William would think what a wonderful woman I was. I wanted to impress them, secretly I've always wanted to impress everyone, even my own children.

JANE: I know.

NANCY: I've spent all my life trying to control things ... keep everything calm ... life at a distance. When Josie talks about sex I feel pinched and crabbed and *jealous* ... that sexual desire and sexual experience, that melting ... I've put myself out in the cold like an Eskimo grandmother ... Hold me [*They embrace.*] And you? You were happy?

JANE: What do you think?

NANCY: Well, I never met David, but in the photographs you look as if you're having a wonderful time — Greece, India!

JANE: We travelled — six months in a kibbutz in Israel, four months in India — Greece — we smoked dope with our friends but — and *don't laugh*, less than a year after we were married David started screwing other women. Staying out half the night. I was desperate, lying awake listening for the sound of his Lambretta, we were living in Rome at that time, teaching English. I pretended I didn't mind. Jealousy wasn't 'in' then — remember? It was the new free love revival. So I just clamped up! I faked the orgasms, I didn't feel a thing, when I left him I told him the truth.

[*She stiffens her body.*]

NANCY: What did he say?

JANE: At first he thought I was just trying to hurt him, but in the end he believed it. He was shattered ... He cried like a baby when I said I couldn't bear it any longer, it was over and I was leaving him. "But you're the only one I've ever loved, the others were nothing to me, I

can't even remember their names." So it
wasn't so hot then and it isn't so hot now ... I
buy myself flowers, I play myself music — But
it isn't enough! I want to be loved!

[NANCY *holds her.*]

NANCY: I'm going to put my house up for sale. What
do you think of that?

[JANE *moves away.*]

JANE: I think that sounds great! Go for what you
want, Nancy! We must put up a fight, even if
we lose, we'll go down fighting. I'm going to
carry on living the way I want ... then if someone comes along who has the same ideas —
then Wow! Pow!

NANCY: I'm going to do more than that — I want to let
the sunshine in — I'm looking for a man, I
want to do some fucking!

[*A voice is heard outside.* VIOLET, JOSIE *and*
DAWN *are returning. The door flies open and in
they come.* MRS MEADOW *sits up in bed.* JANE
and NANCY *stand. There is a pause, a moment's
silence as the women face each other.*]

VIOLET: We lost! The bastards are going to close it!

NANCY: What happened?

VIOLET: You could tell. Whatever we said they'd got
their minds made up.

JANE: Here, sit down. I'll make some tea.

JOSIE: The bastards!

MRS MEADOW: Thank God you brought Dawn back, I knew it
would be too much excitement!

[*She opens a bottle of pills and goes towards*
DAWN.]

DAWN: Not now, Mother — later! They're going to
lock the doors, Mother, and not let us in any
more!

MRS MEADOW: Now don't get all aerated, Dawn! See what
you've done, she's all aerated!

DAWN: It's not fair. They've upset Violet! Not now, Mother — later.

[*She pushes away the pills.*]

JANE: How soon are they going to close?

VIOLET: Three weeks — three bloody weeks —

NANCY: I brought a bottle of champagne in hoping we might be going to celebrate. Shall we drink it?

VIOLET: Open it up, there's a good girl. I don't want no tea this evening.

[NANCY *opens the champagne.* JANE *gets some glasses* — JOSIE *is sitting, very depressed.* NANCY *takes her over some champagne.*]

JOSIE: So, what'll we bloody toast?

NANCY: To our baths!

VIOLET: Hey Nancy, you're going to make me cry.

ALL: To our baths!

NANCY: How was your speech, Josie?

JANE: Did you speak too, Violet?

DAWN: I spoke, I told them if they closed the baths, they'd have to put me and Mother in a home!

MRS MEADOW: You didn't get up on no platform, did you Dawn?

DAWN: Yes I did, I took the mike and I spoke up!

MRS MEADOW: Dawn, I told you, never speak to strangers!

VIOLET: My husband spoke up! "What's going to happen to me?" I asks. "Staff over fifty are to be offered an early retirement," one of them says. "Retire her!" my husband shouts out. "After eighteen years service with not one day for sickness lost, how can you justify that?"

JANE: So he stuck up for you?

VIOLET: Well, he had to, didn't he? Between ourselves, he's been getting a bit jealous lately — can't believe there isn't some fellow behind us. [*laughs*] I enjoy a bit of jealousy ... I tease him ... egg him on ... I can always tell when he's jealous — his toes curl up —

JOSIE: I bet he's hot stuff, Violet!

VIOLET: He is when I get him going!

[*Meanwhile* JOSIE *has been taking her clothes off and wrapping herself in a towel.*]

NANCY: So what did you say, Josie?

VIOLET: Josie was the star. She was the star of the occasion.

JOSIE: Bloody hopeless!

JANE: What did you say?

[JOSIE *walks to the centre of the stage and improvises a mike.*]

JOSIE: Ladies and gentlemen, I am here this evening to put the case of the Turkish Baths before you. The architect has advised, due to deterioration, £75,000 will have to be spent. If you look at that figure in relation to the £11,000 spent on fireworks this year, plus the number of O.A.P.s who haven't got a bath at home or who, if they have, can't afford to heat the water, it might appear this was a service the self-respecting ratepayer was happy to provide ...

DAWN: They tried to upset her ...

VIOLET: They tried to confuse her ...

JOSIE: They threw figures at me. "It's a matter of money," they said. "Don't say it's a matter of money — it's a matter of the way you divide the money," I says. "You're proposing to spend four million pounds on a new library with this and that and the other and you can't find £75,000 to mend our baths." As I was speaking I kept thinking, this can't be me saying all this with all these people listening ... this can't be Josie, she'd never dare ... then one of them says to me "Madam, you're living in cuckoo-land — no commercial enterprise would provide what you propose." Well, that done it, it's now or never, girl, speak your

mind ... so I goes on, "We are of the opinion
that this Council has taken a liberty and
jumped the gun by closing our baths without
consulting us and by golly we aren't going to
let you get away with it. You know it's not the
money. It's not that at all, you know it's not.
It's personal grandisement of the blokes at the
top — it makes them feel *big* ... to spend all
that money — so important they can probably
ask to have their wages boosted into the bargain
... I mean, men that are in charge of all that
cash, well, they must be very important people,
mustn't they? But what I'm here tonight to tell
you is that we are important too!

NANCY: Bravo Josie! Bravo!

JOSIE: And so are the pensioners and so are the blind
and so are the ordinary men and women who
have been coming to these baths all their lives,
for a swim or a laundry or to get together in a
bit of steam to relax and pass the time
together...

VIOLET: She said it all just like that ... anyone would
think she'd been doing it all her life ...

JOSIE: So then all the men and the women sitting
round the table — they voted on it ... proposal
to repair and give us six months to get atten-
dance up ...

[*Pause.*]

VIOLET: And we lost. They turned us down! Just like
that! "Out!" they said, "Three weeks then
out!"

[BILL*'s voice can be heard shouting down the
stairs.*]

BILL: [*off*] Nine o'clock ladies! Get yourselves
moving!

JOSIE: No! Why bleeding well should I! I'm staying!

JANE: What d'you mean?

JOSIE: I mean I'm staying here! I'm going to occupy
          — that all right by you, Violet?

VIOLET: All right by me! I'm staying with you — they
          can drag me out before I walk! [*She marches to
          the door and shouts up.*] You can lock up, Bill,
          we're staying!

BILL: [*off*] What's that?

VIOLET: I said you can lock up and go home. We're
          staying!

          [*The sound of* BILL *coming down the stairs.*
          VIOLET *slams the door and slips the bolt.*]

          Now get through that, Houdini! Who's for
          leaving better get going quick!

          [BILL *rattles on the door, his face against the
          glass.*]

BILL: [*off*] Violet! Violet, you there?

VIOLET: Stand back from the glass, Bill Bradley, I
          know what you're after!

JANE: Is your telephone working, Violet?

VIOLET: Yes.

JANE: Right, I'll just make a call to see if Sam can
          stay the night next door. Then I'm staying.

NANCY: There's no-one waiting for me at home. I'm
          staying.

BILL: Hurry up, ladies, and vacate these premises!

DAWN: Oh, let us stay, Mother. Please! Please!

MRS MEADOW: You behave yourself, Dawn!

DAWN: Please!

MRS MEADOW: Oh, all right, we'll stay too, Violet and back
          you up.

BILL: [*off*] What's going on in there, Violet, have
          you all gone mad or something?

VIOLET: No darling — we're occupying our baths!

BILL: [*off*] You'll never get away with this, Violet.

VIOLET: Who says!

          [*The sound of* BILL *going back upstairs.*]

JOSIE: For twenty years all I've ever thought about

has been money and clothes and my home —

JANE: And sex —

JOSIE: All right, and sex. I knew nothing about the world — now I'm going to change all that. I'm branching out — I'm going somehow or other to get meself ...

NANCY: *My*self.

JOSIE: ... Myself an education.

VIOLET: Public speaking like that, you'll be on the Council before long ... Here, ladies, what about a steam-up to celebrate?

> [*The stage goes misty as the women begin to undress. As the mist clears we see the 'plunge' pool in the foreground of the stage and hanging above it a Tarzan rope and high board.*]

JOSIE: We can make this place like a palace ... all pink and white marble and plants hanging from the ceiling ... and a hot fountain rising out of the middle of the plunge — Violet could wear a leopard-skin bathing suit and I'd have white satin with a sheen on it.

> [DAWN *bends her knees so that she is almost squatting — suddenly she jumps right up.*]

DAWN: Weeeeeeee.

> [JANE *grabs the loose rope and swings over the pool.*]

JANE: [*thumps her chest; Tarzan call*] Me Jane!

> [*She drops into the water.* NANCY *takes the rope.*]

NANCY: I'm frightened.

> [JANE *holds out her arms.* NANCY *jumps.* JANE *catches her and they gasp and play and splash together.* JOSIE *comes next.*]

JOSIE: I can't swim. I never learnt.

> [NANCY *and* JANE *hold out their arms.* JOSIE *leaps.*]

VIOLET: Hey, ladies. [*She climbs the ladder and stands on the high board.*] Do the Council honestly think they stand a chance against a bunch of trapeze artists such as us?

> [DAWN *climbs up the rope and stands beside her.*]

DAWN: Look, Mother, what I can do!

> [*She swings into the pool and comes up choking.*]

THE END